DUCKS DOING HUMAN THINGS

COLORING BOOK

BY BRANDON BISHOP
& RONALD KOTYNSKI

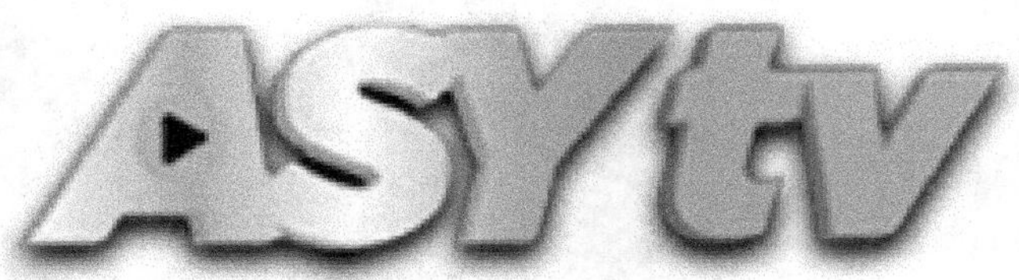

Ducks Doing Human Things Coloring Book

Written and Illustrated by Brandon Bishop & Ronald Kotynski

Published by Burning Bulb Publishing, P.O. Box 4721, Bridgeport, WV 26330
ISBN: 978-1-948278-78-2

DUCKS DOING HUMAN THINGS

The Coloring Book by Brandon Bishop & Ronald Kotynski

Everything is all about parallel universes and infinite dimensions these days. Well, if that's the case, then I am 100% certain that there's a timeline somewhere within the cosmos where ducks, yes DUCKS, are the most dominant species on the planet, and they dress like and act like we humans do in our current dimension…

Okay, we just wanted to see what ducks would look like doing human things. (Do we really have to explain it?)

Get your crayons and markers out, and let's bring this duck universe to life!

I wonder what other animals we can dress up and put to work…

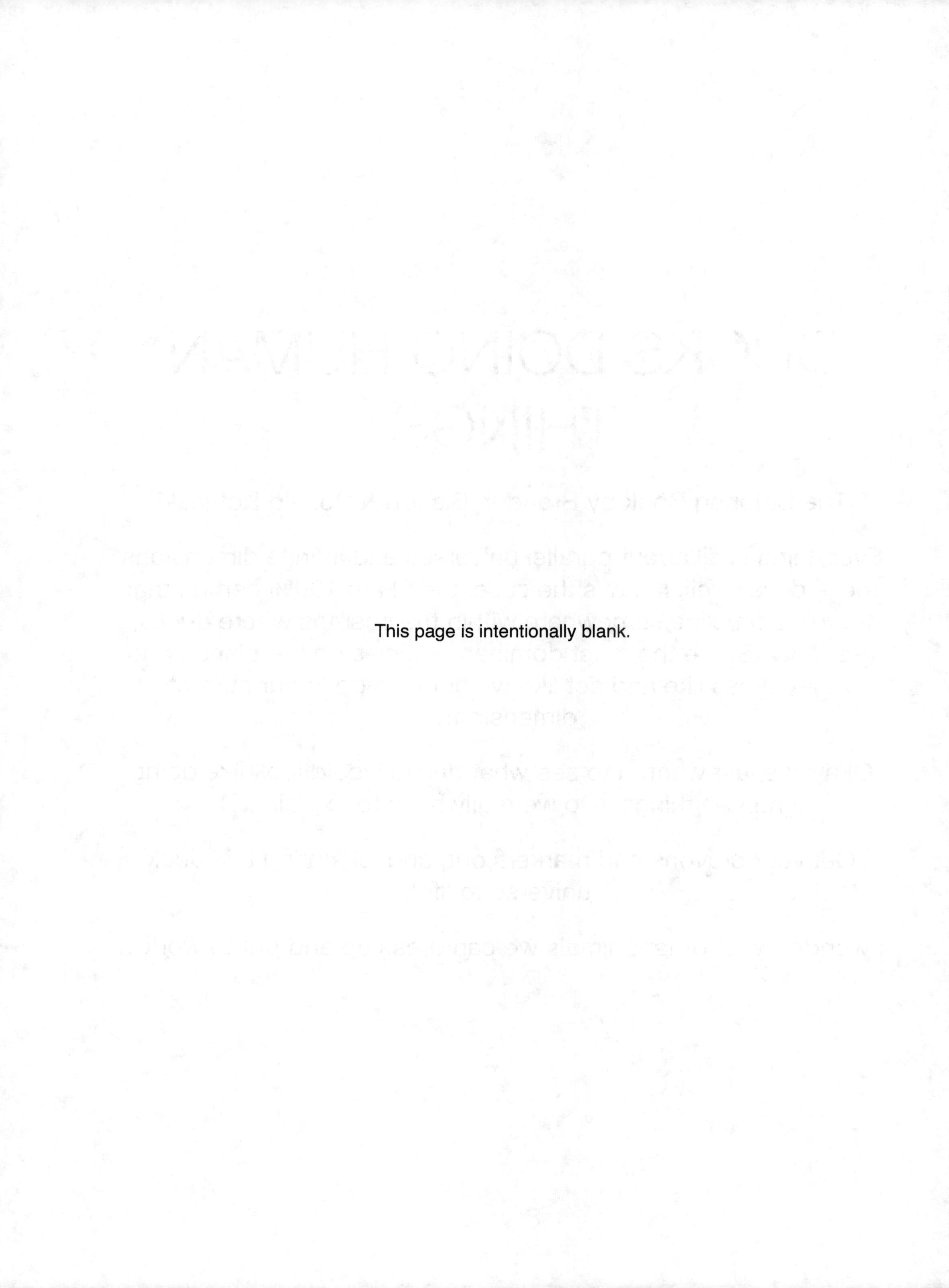

This page is intentionally blank.

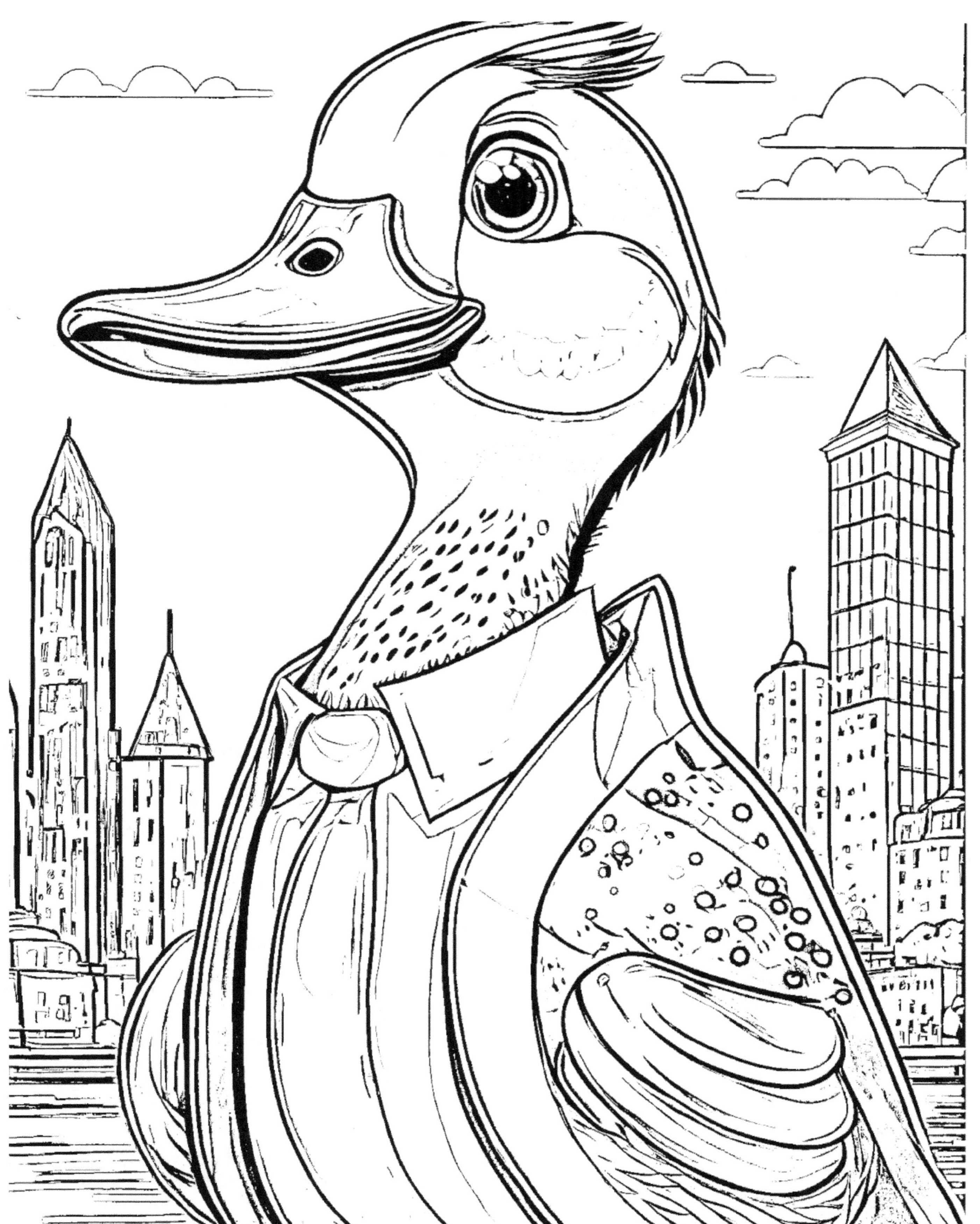

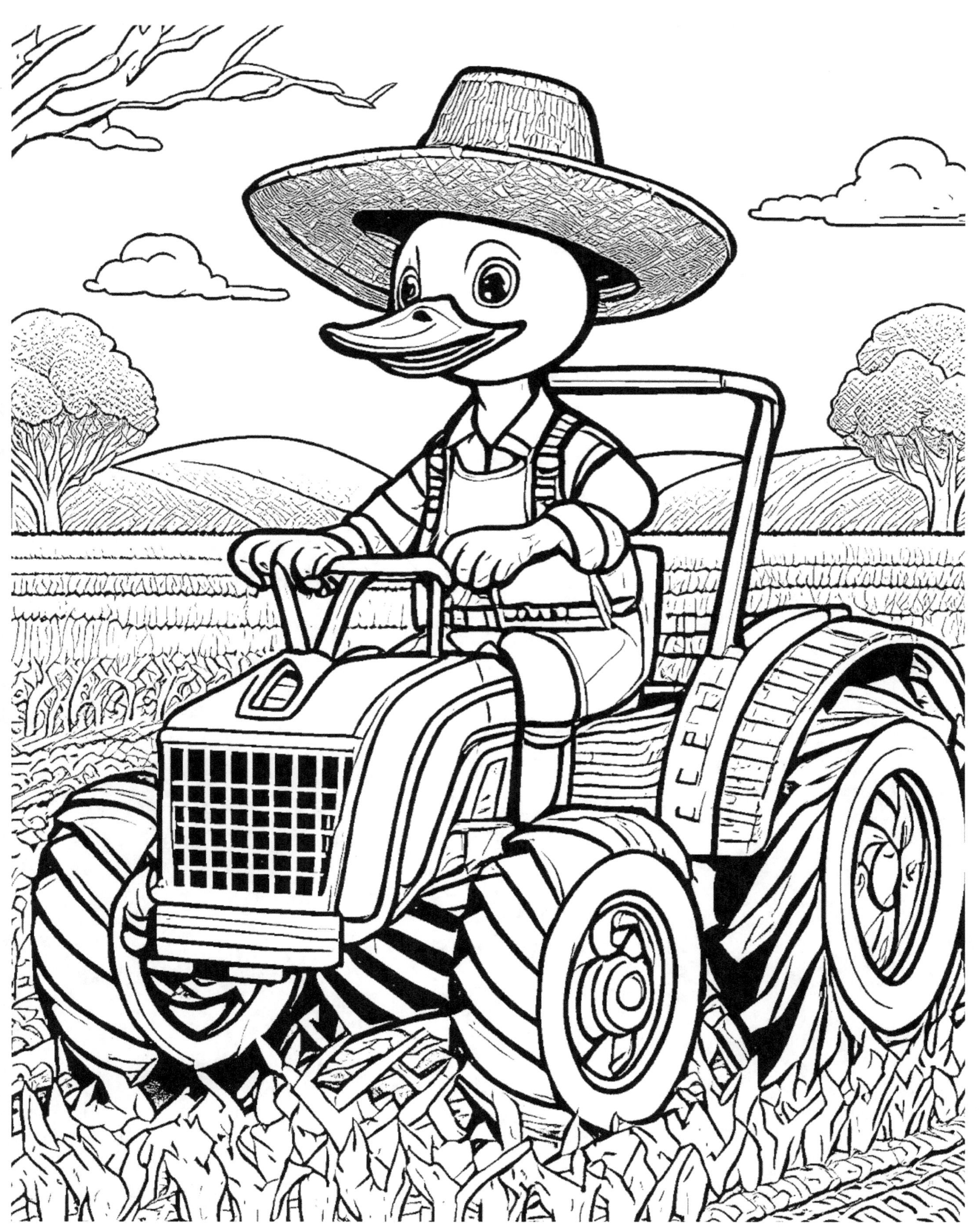

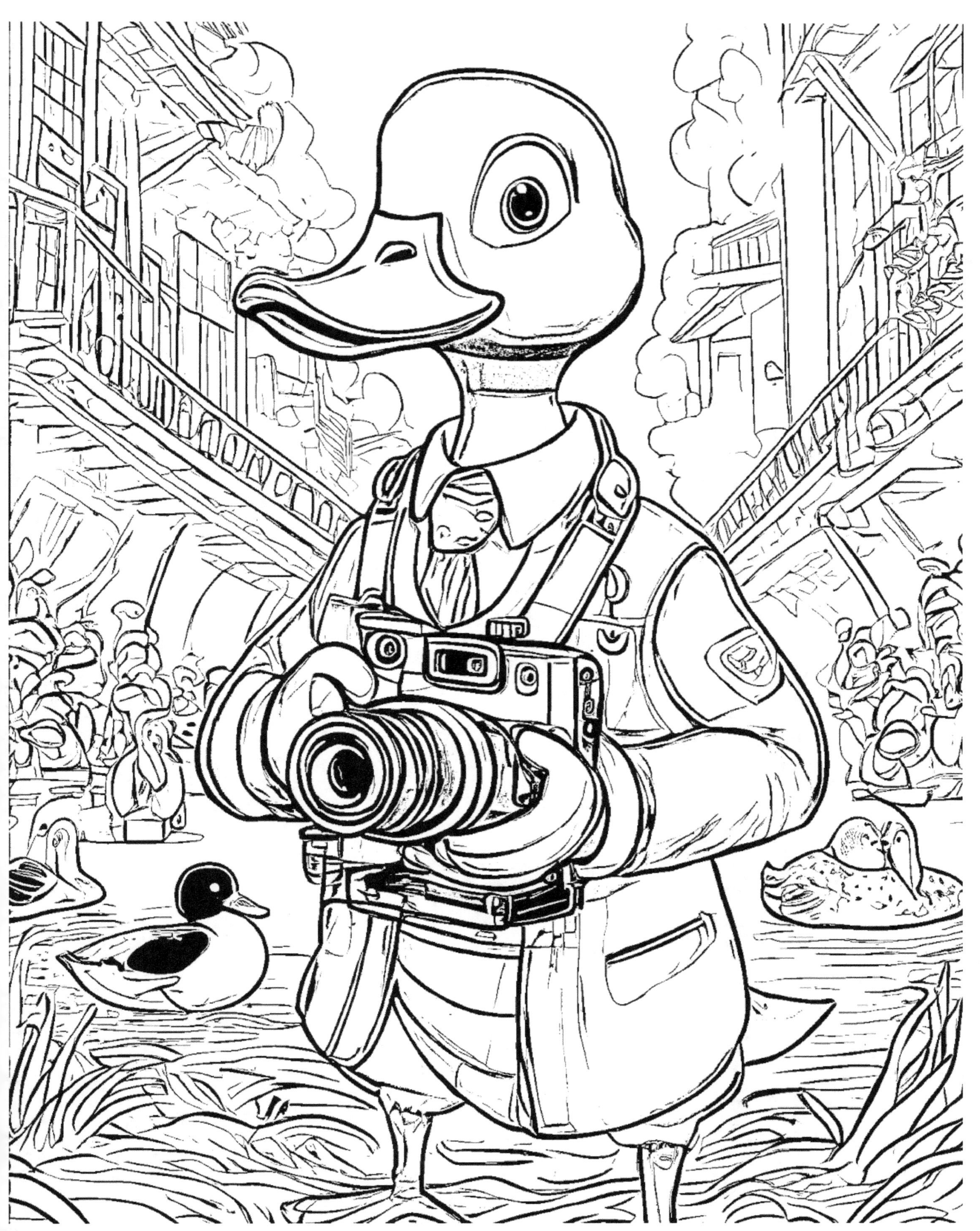

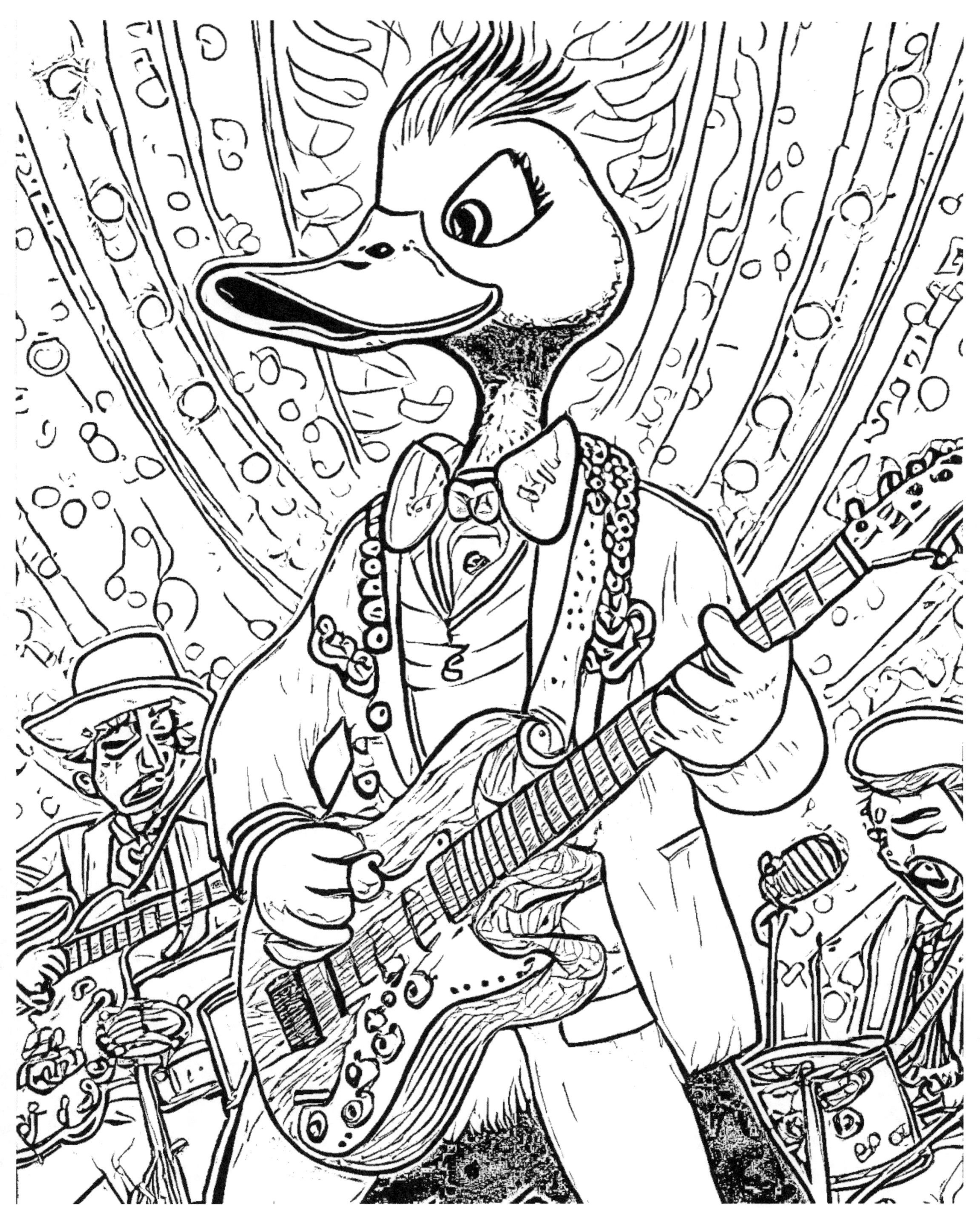

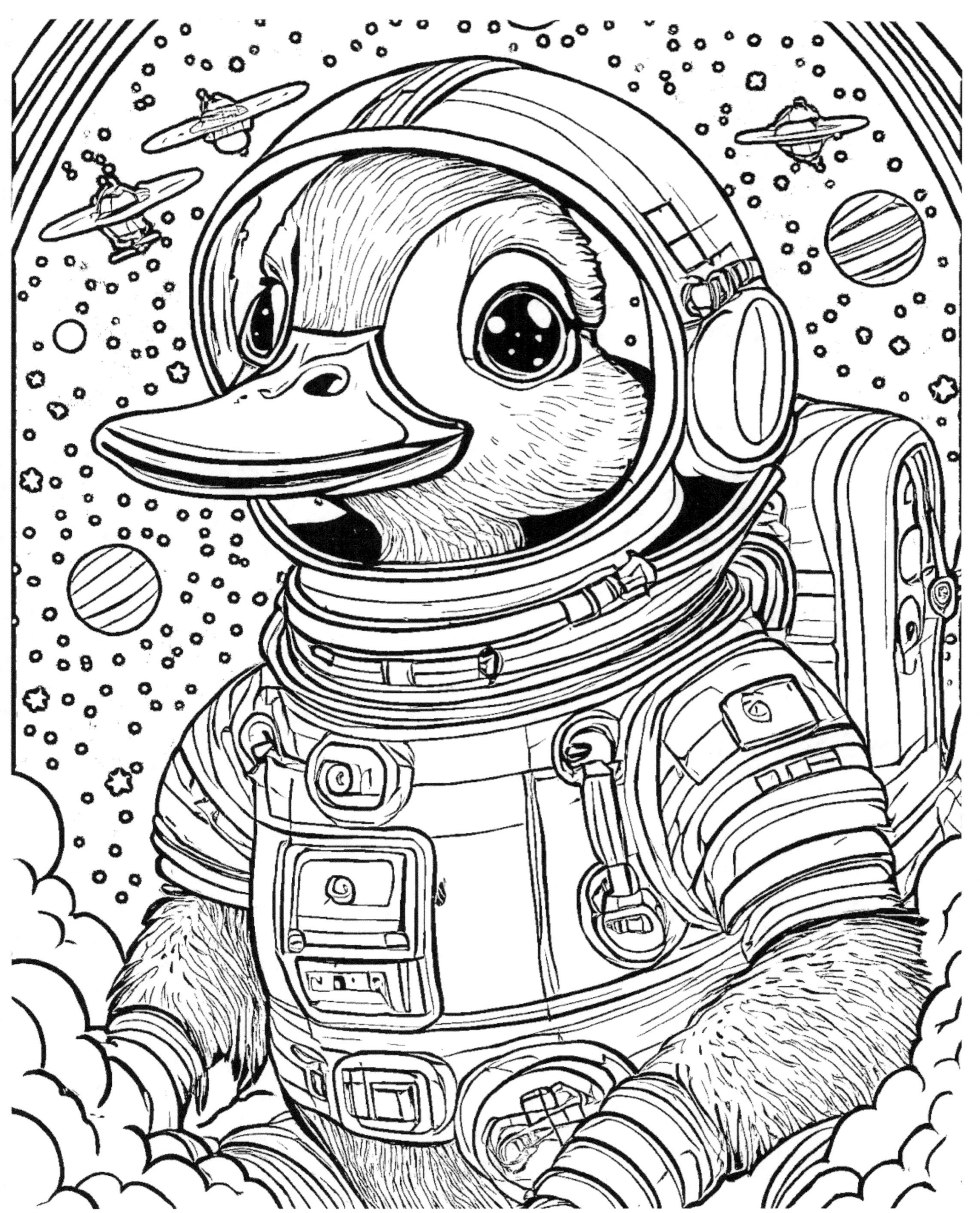

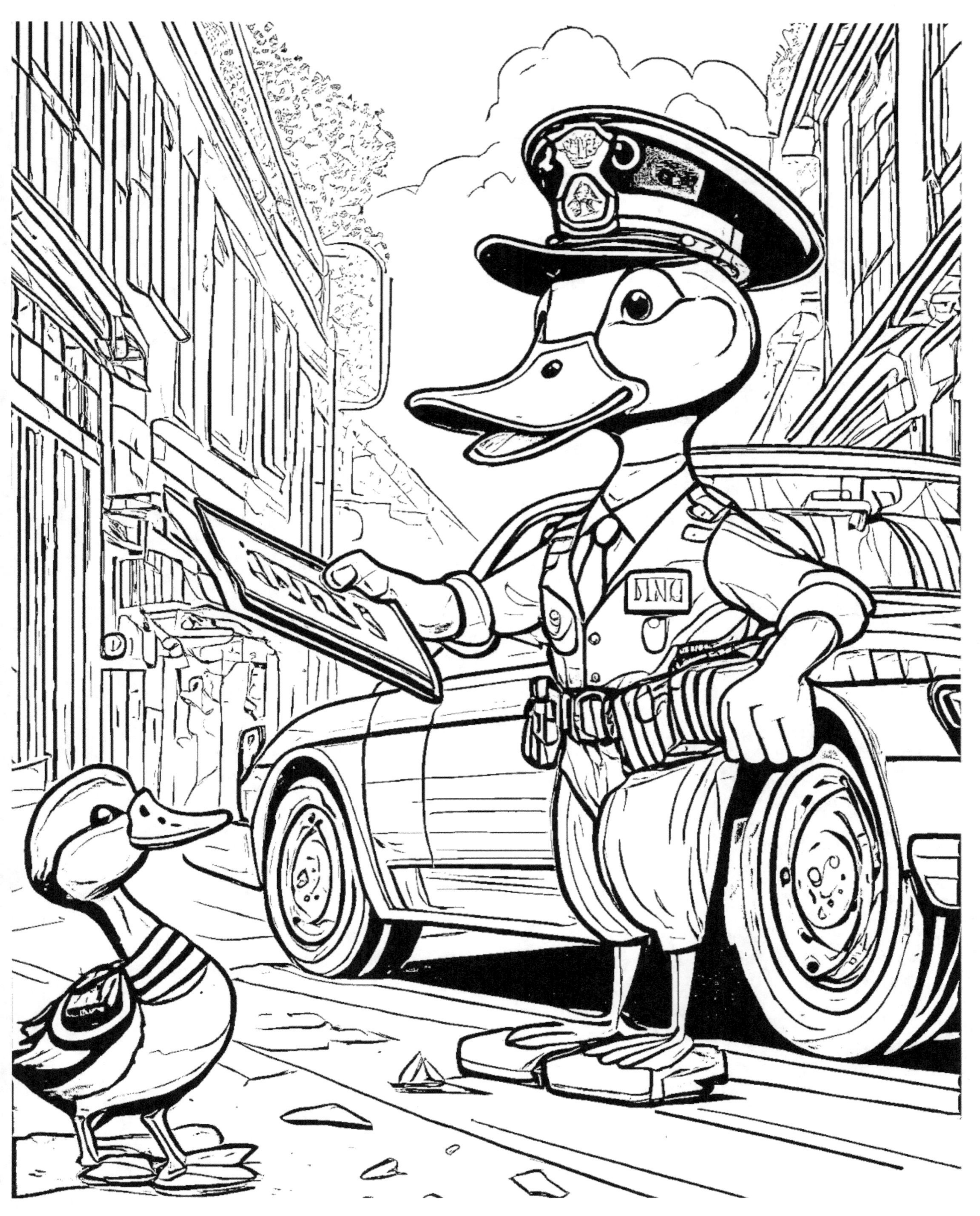

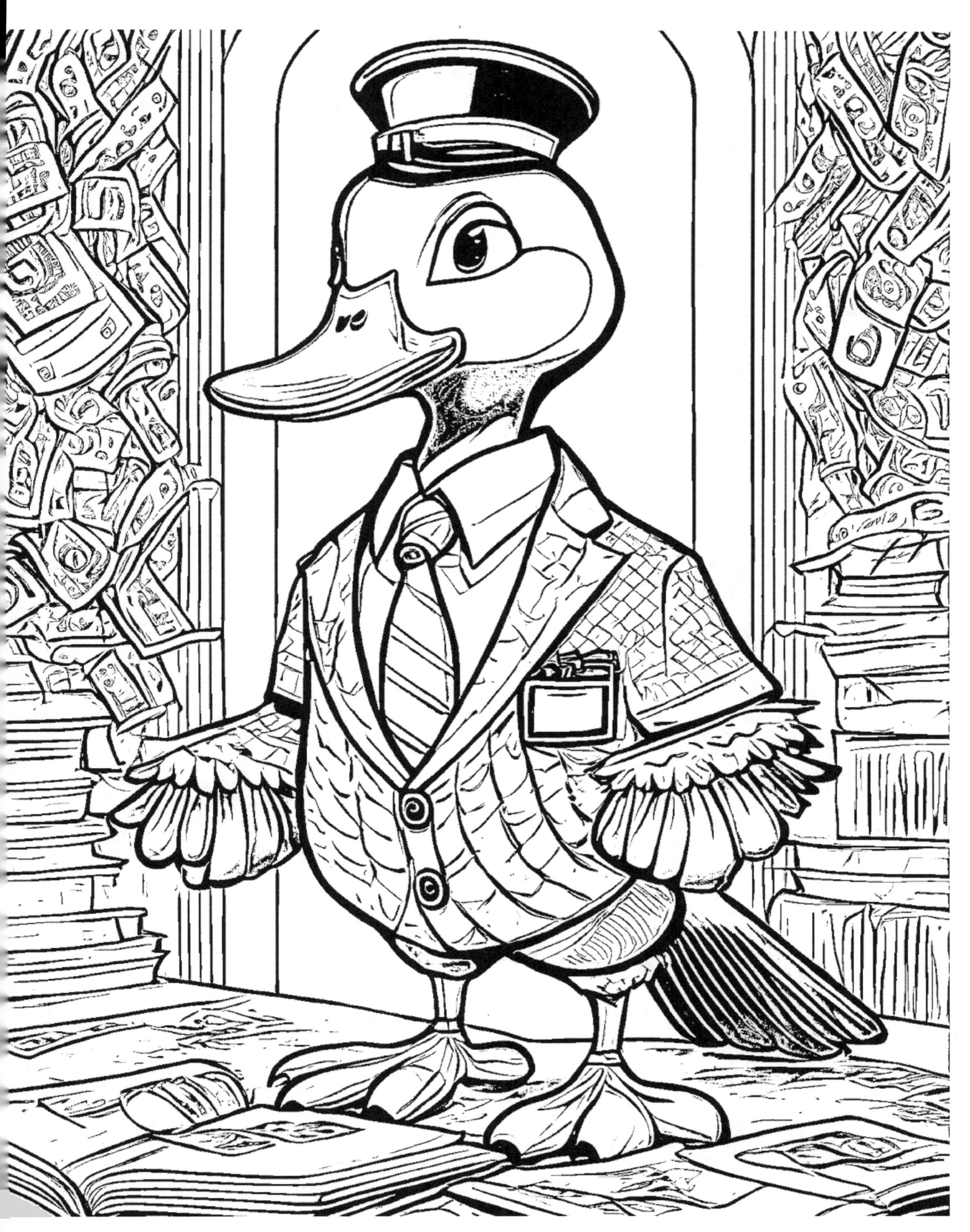

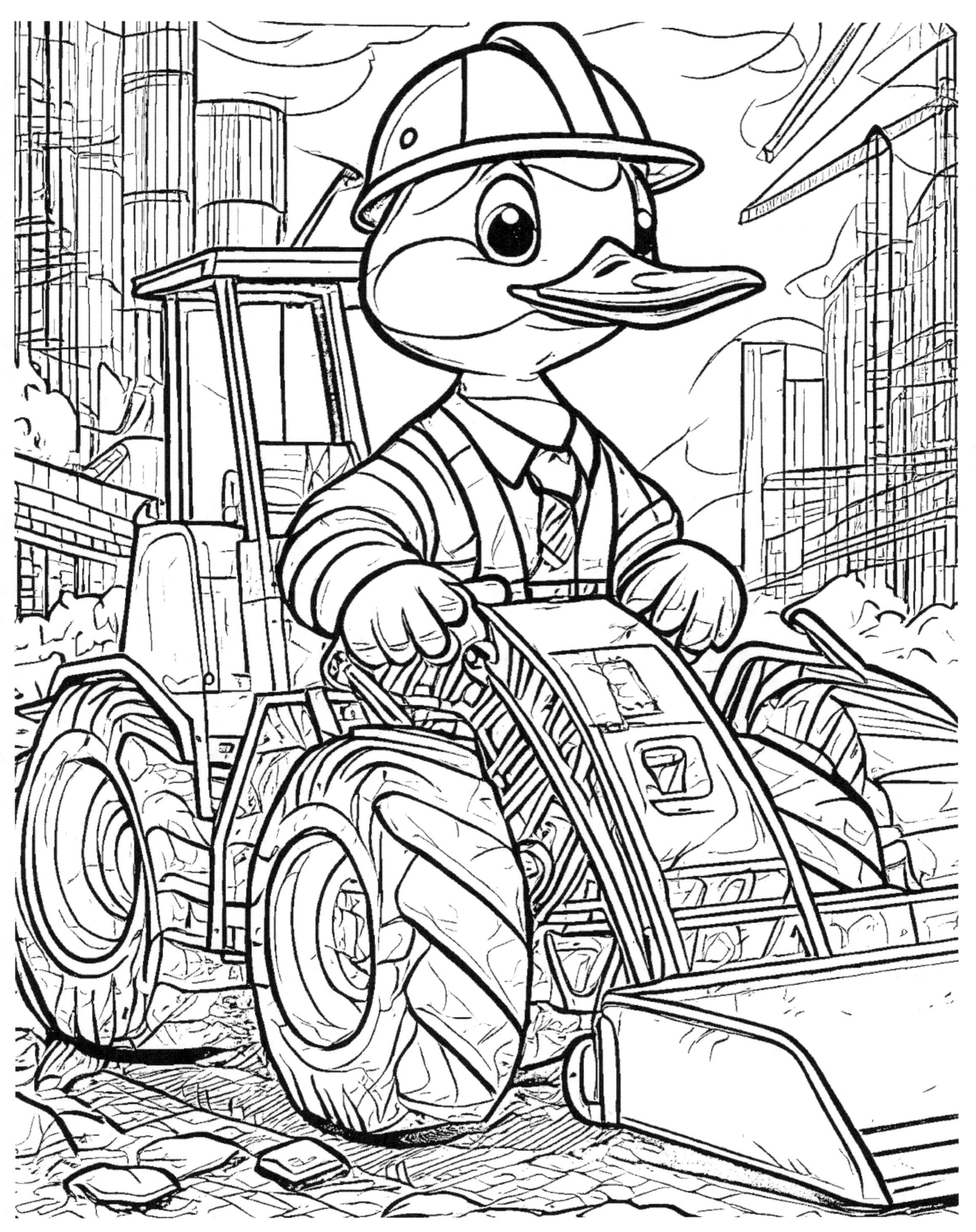

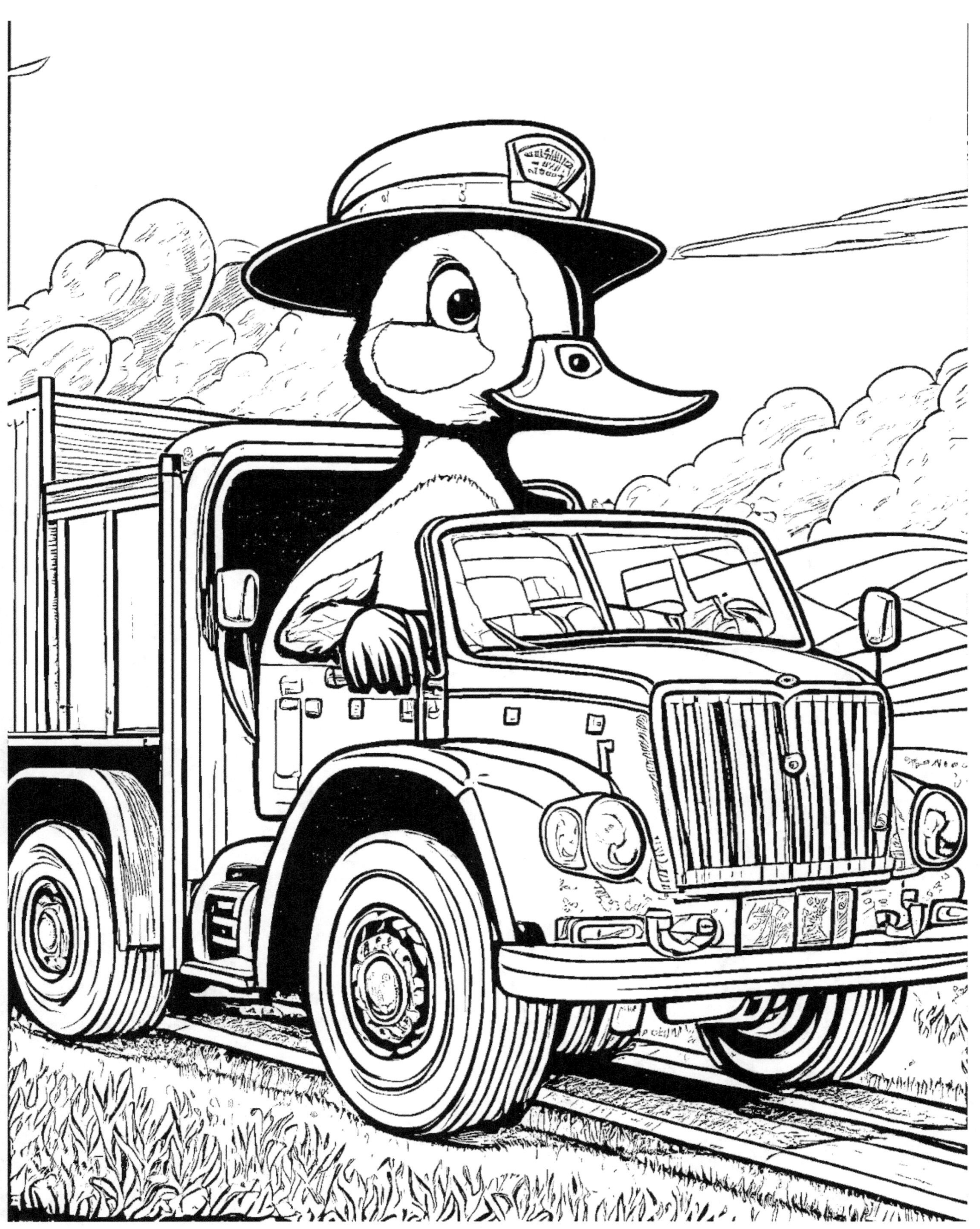

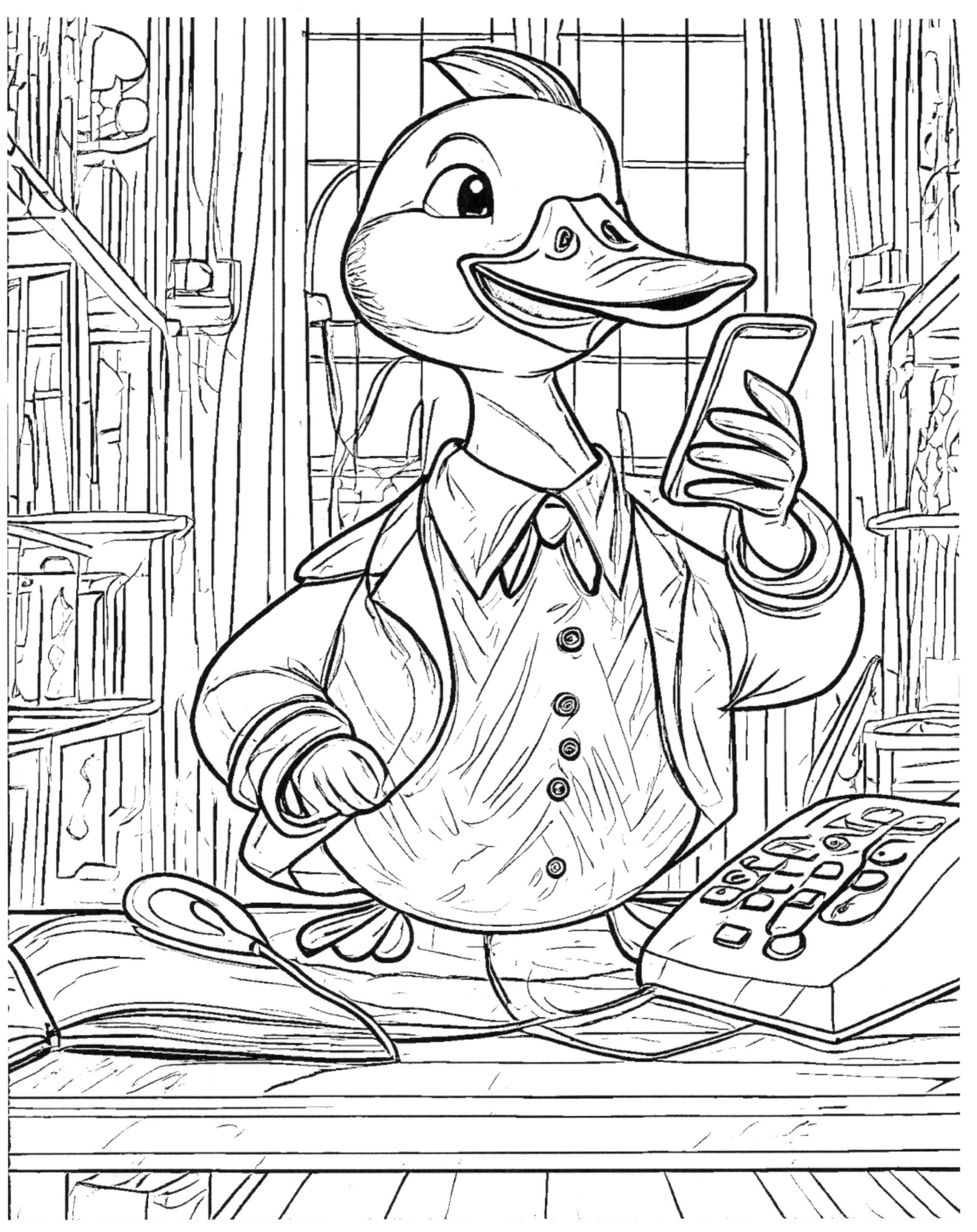

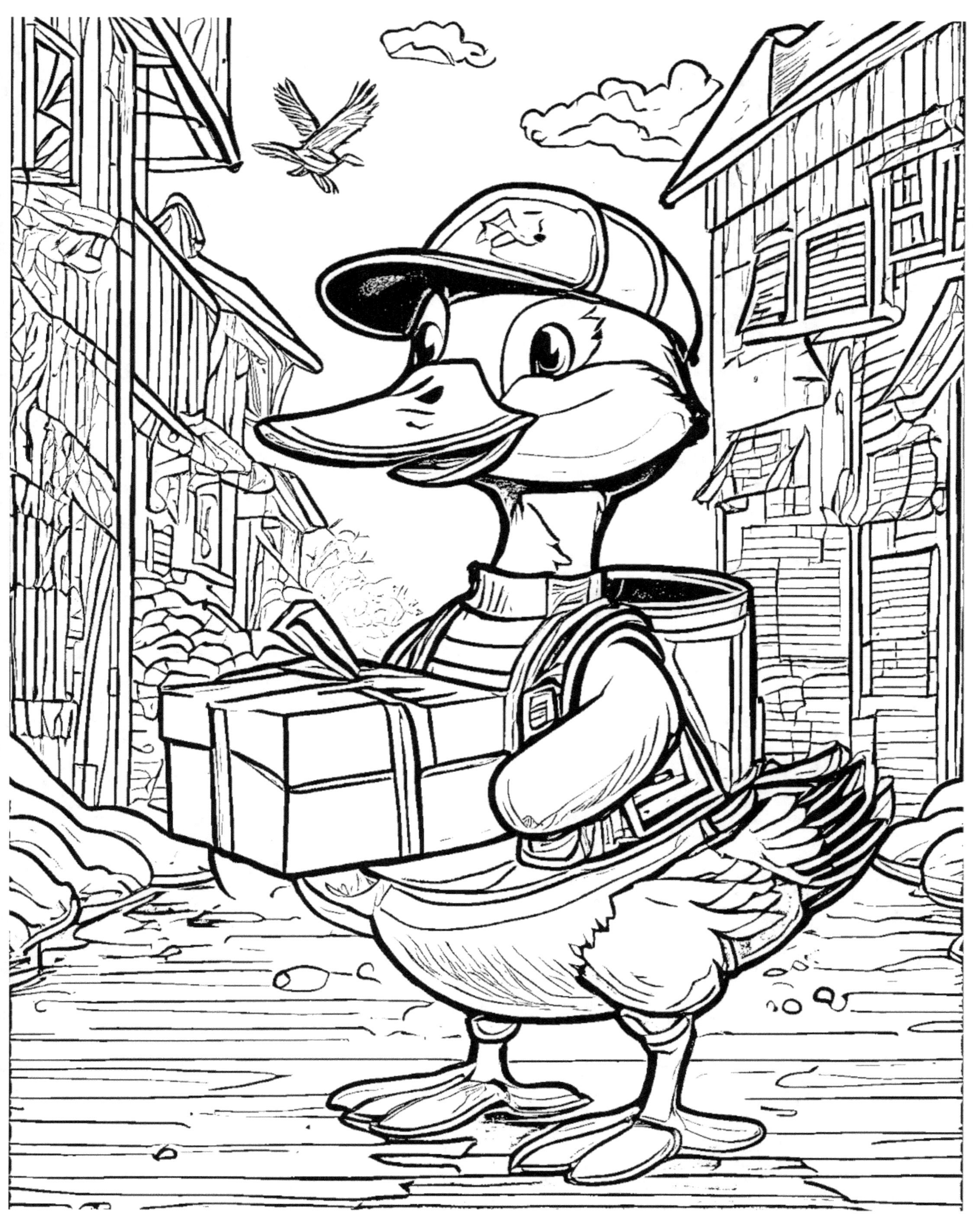

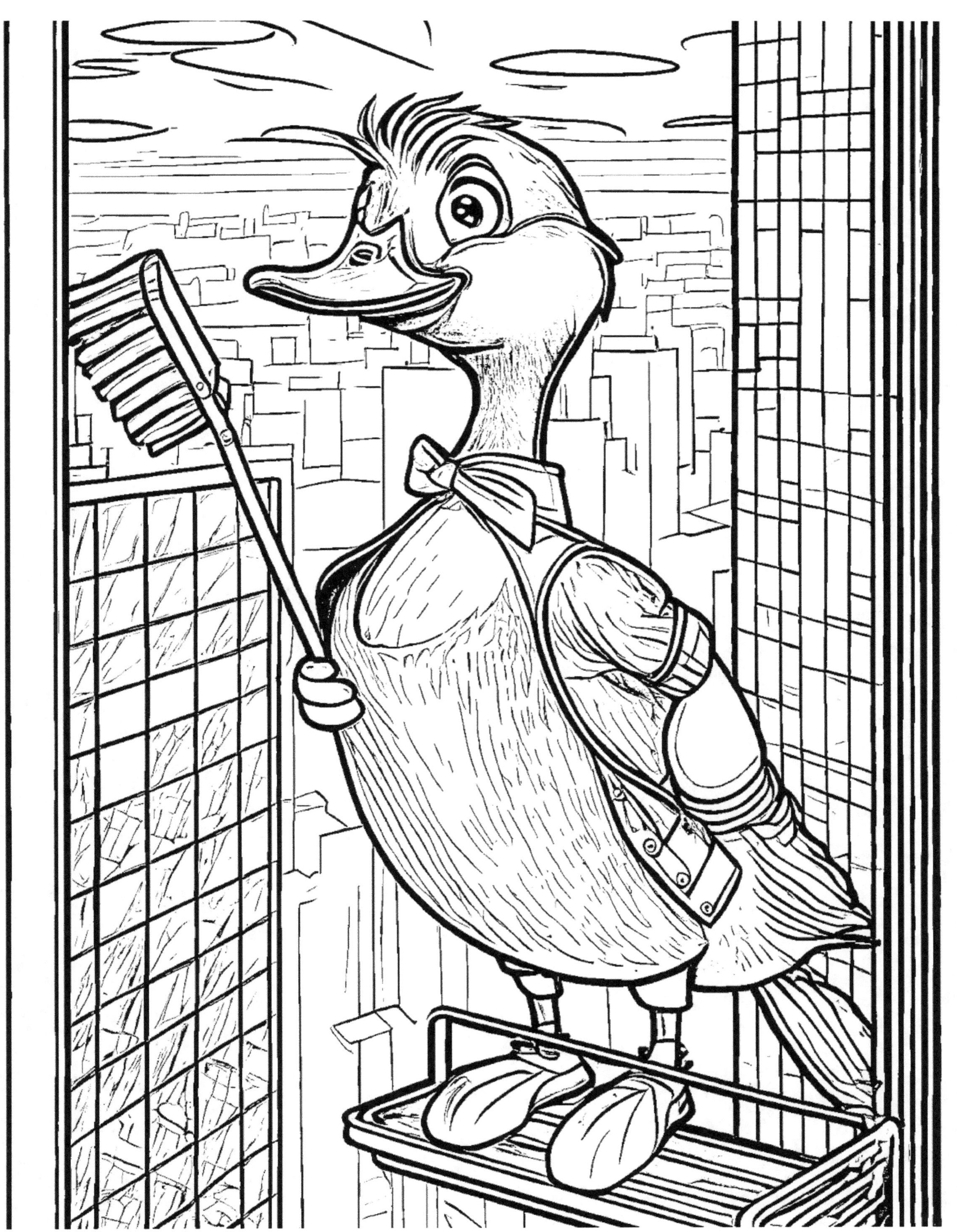

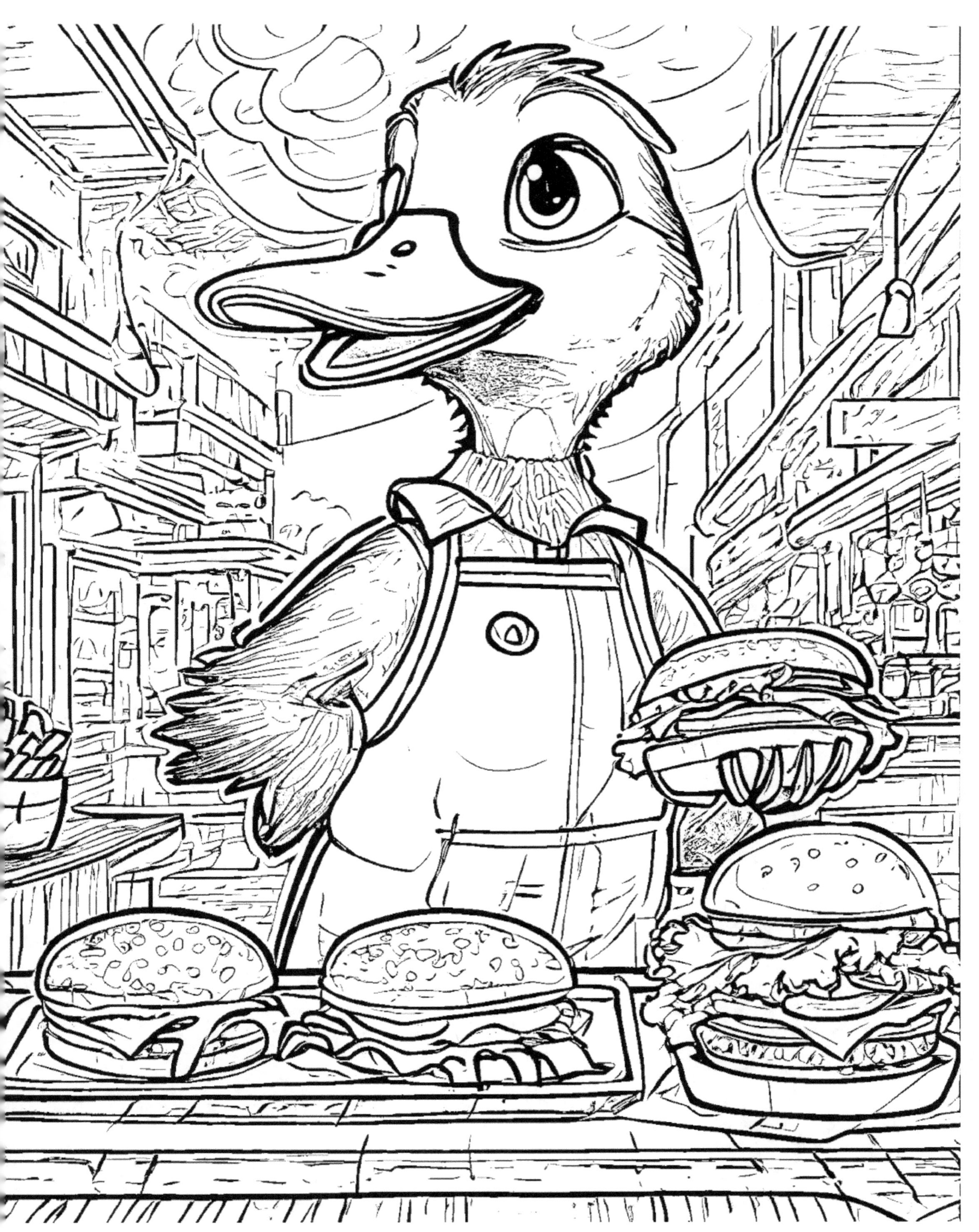

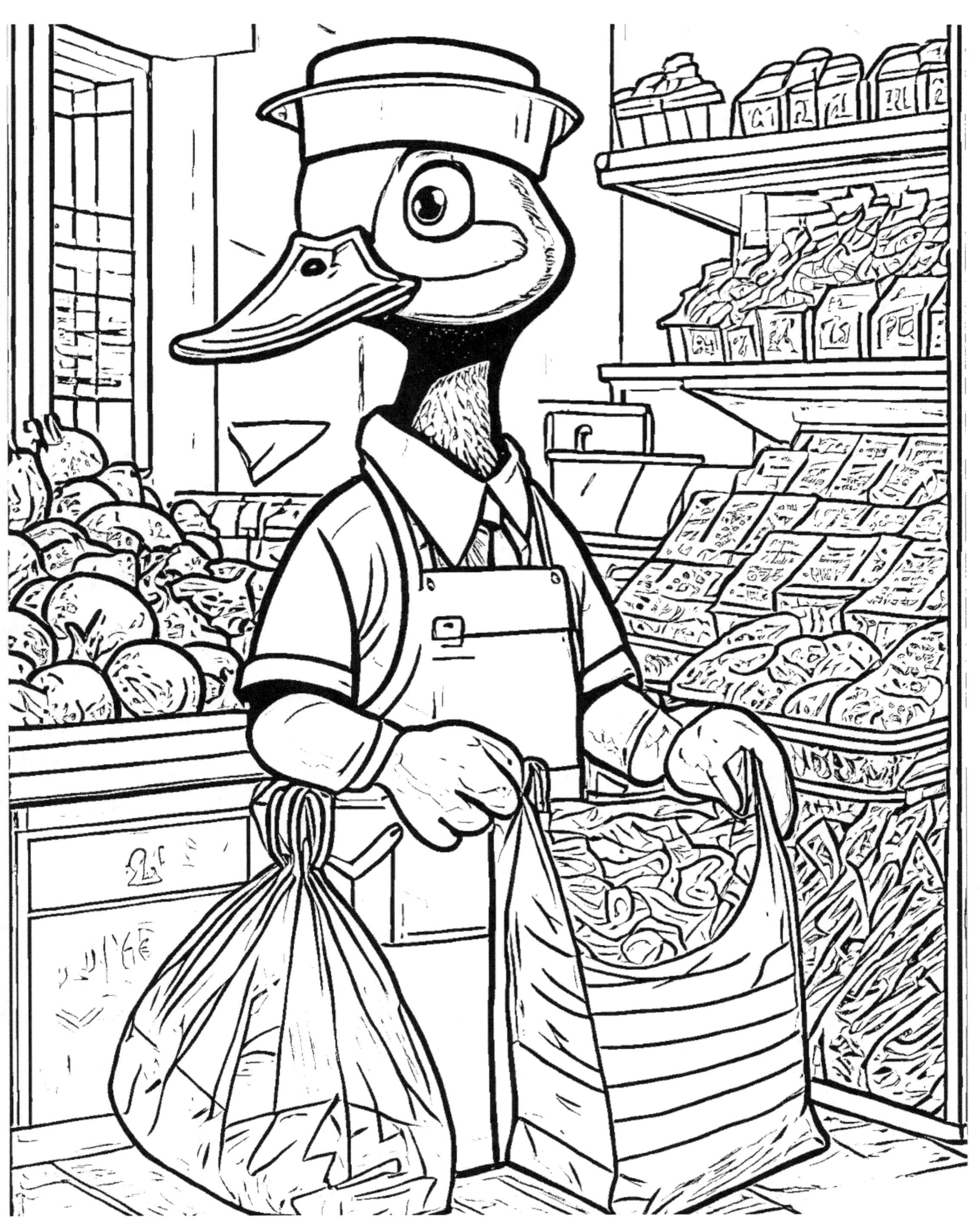

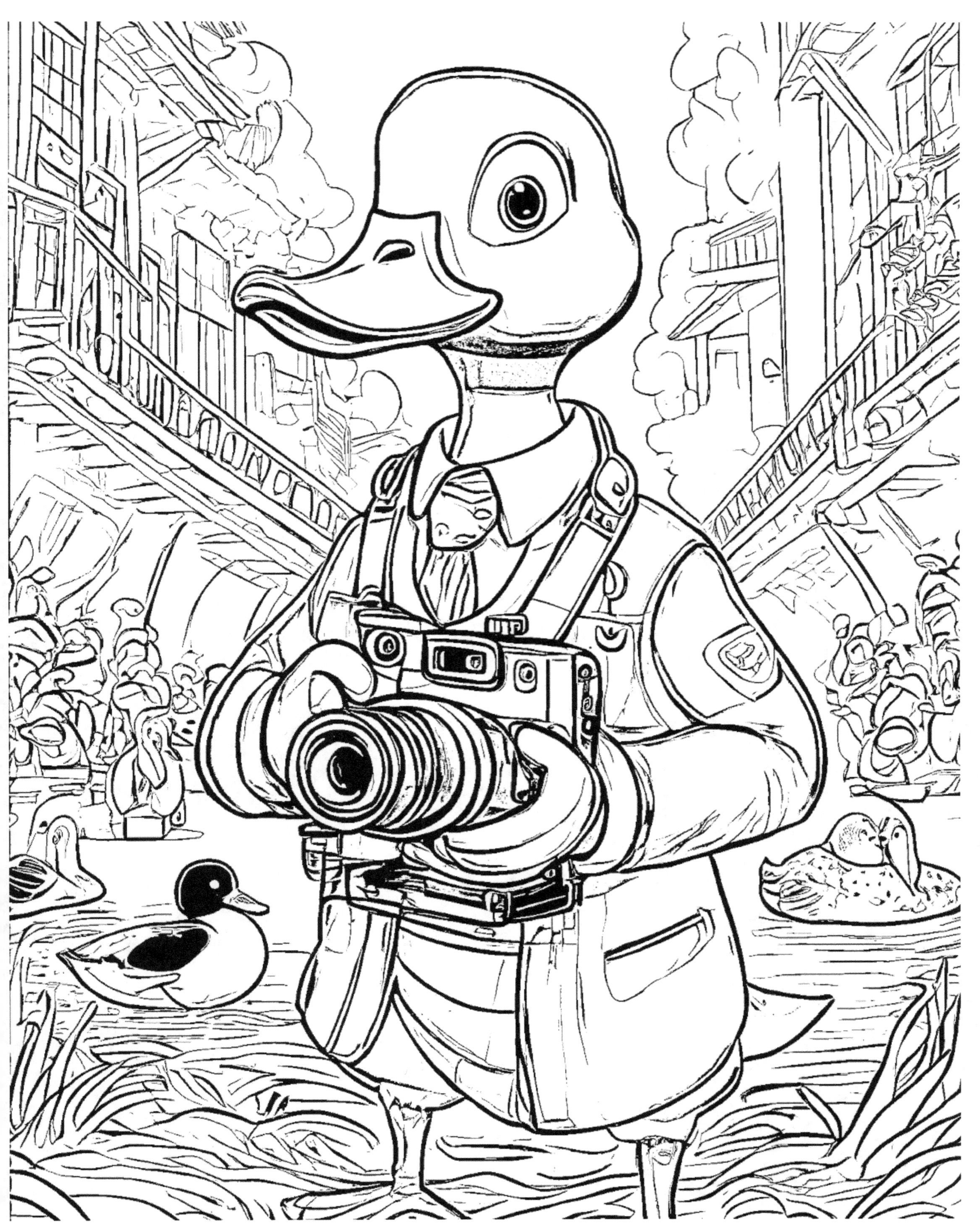

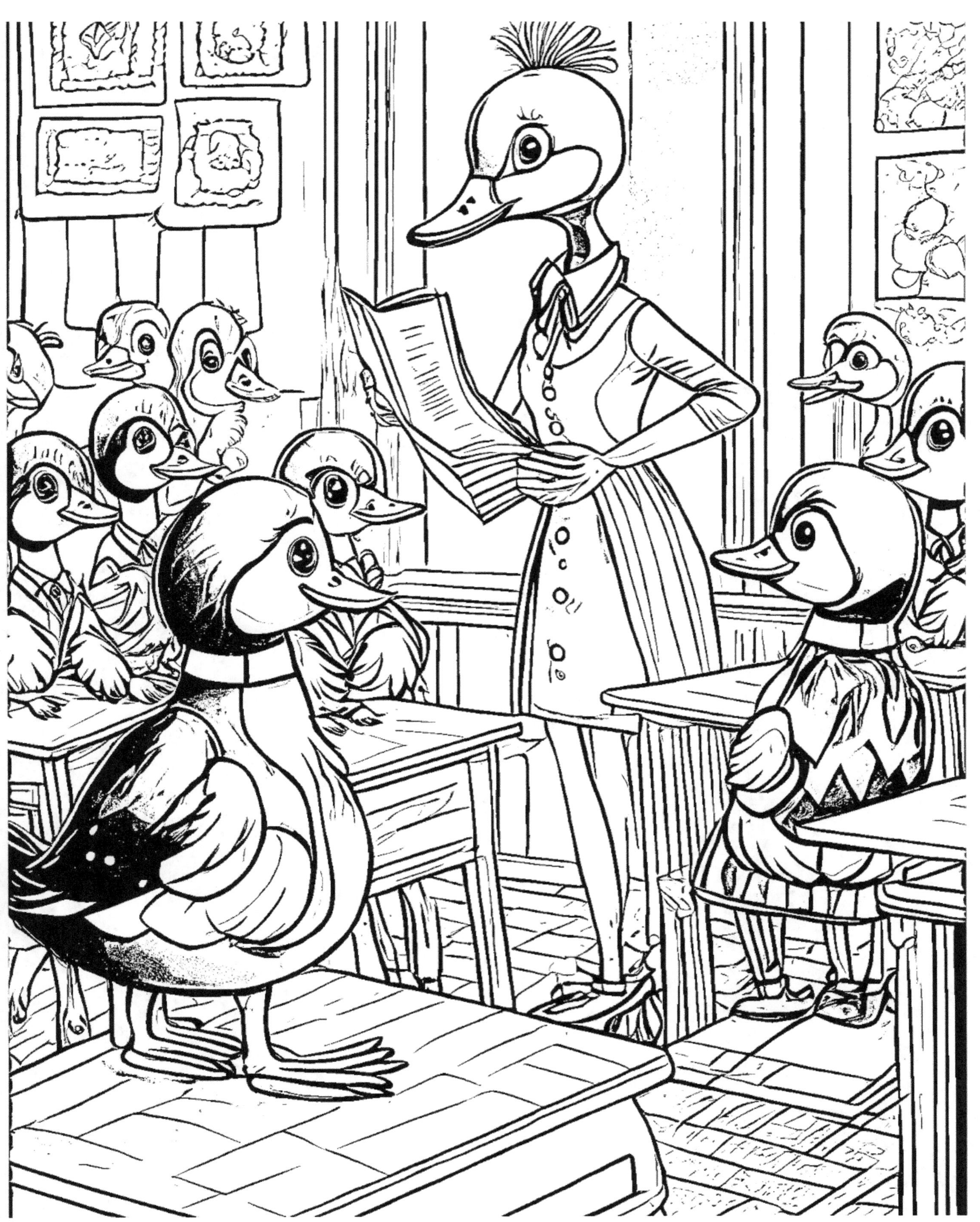

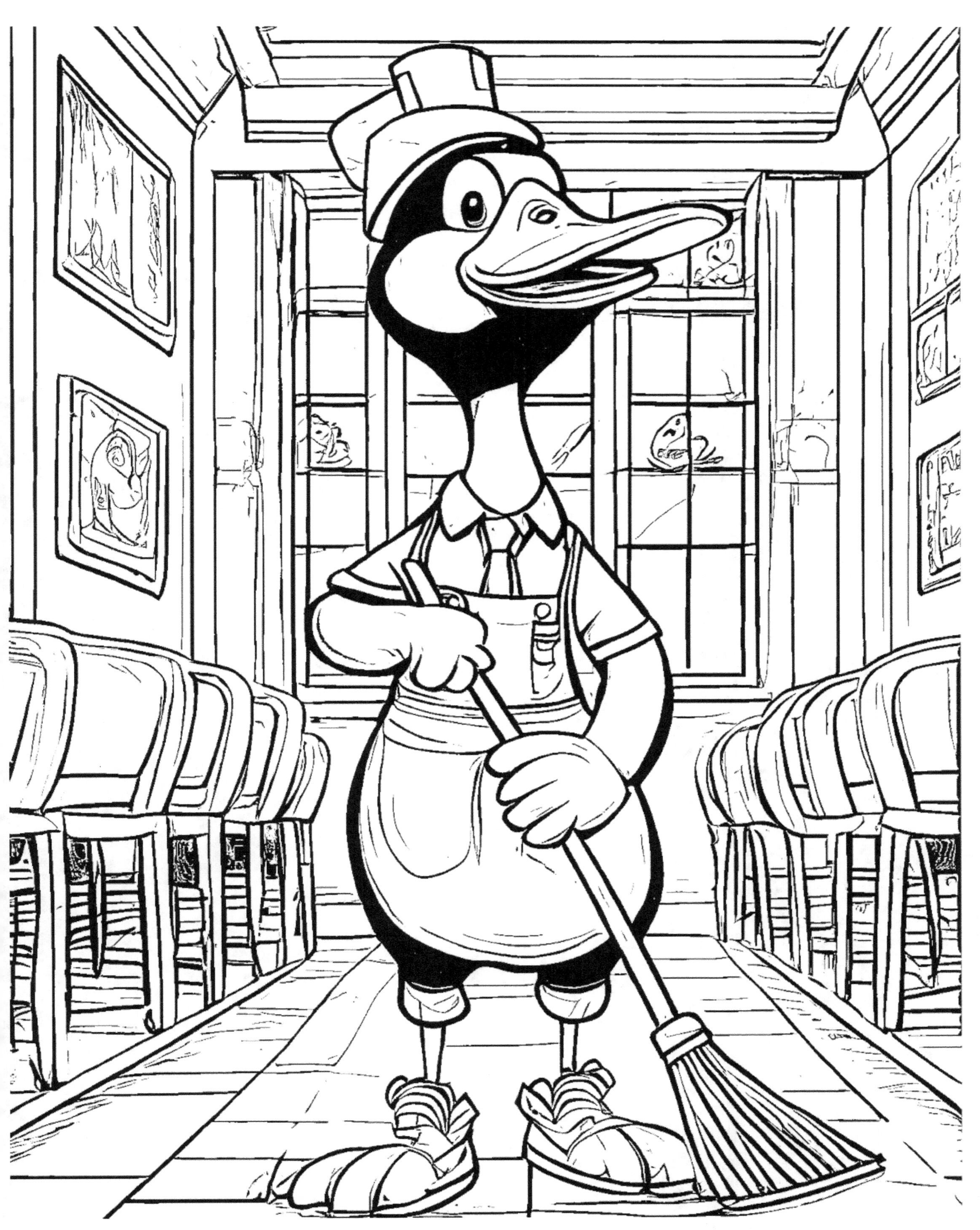

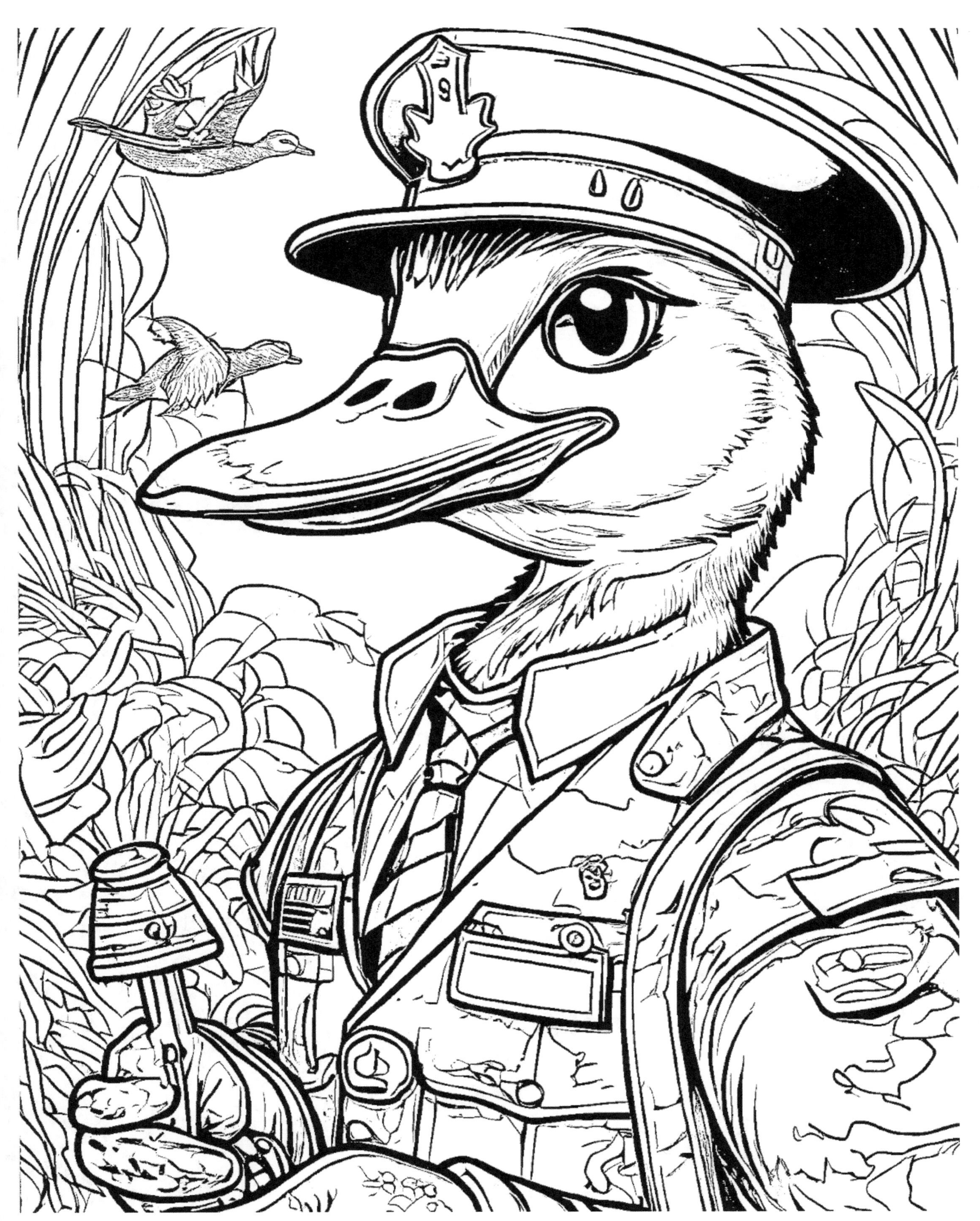

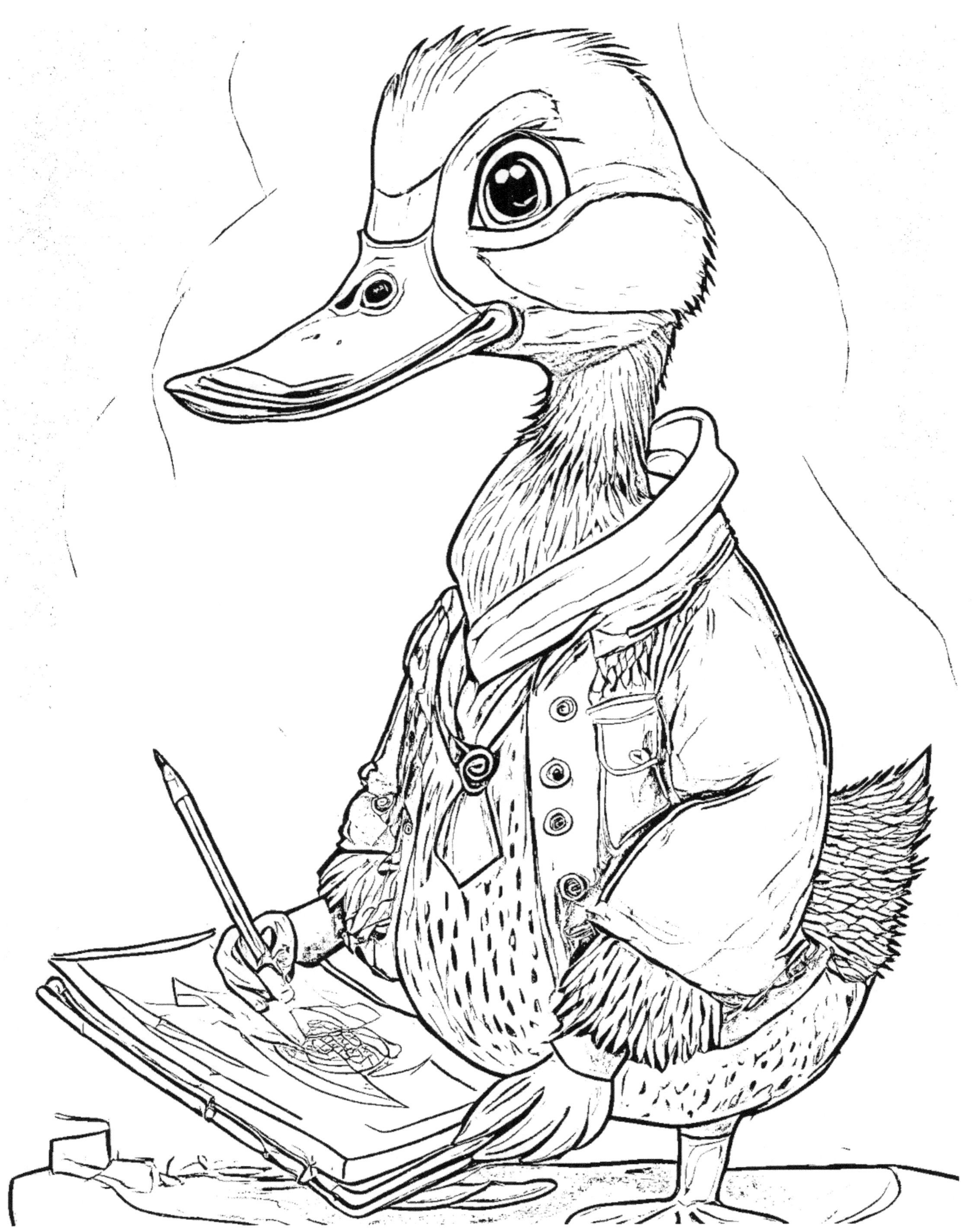

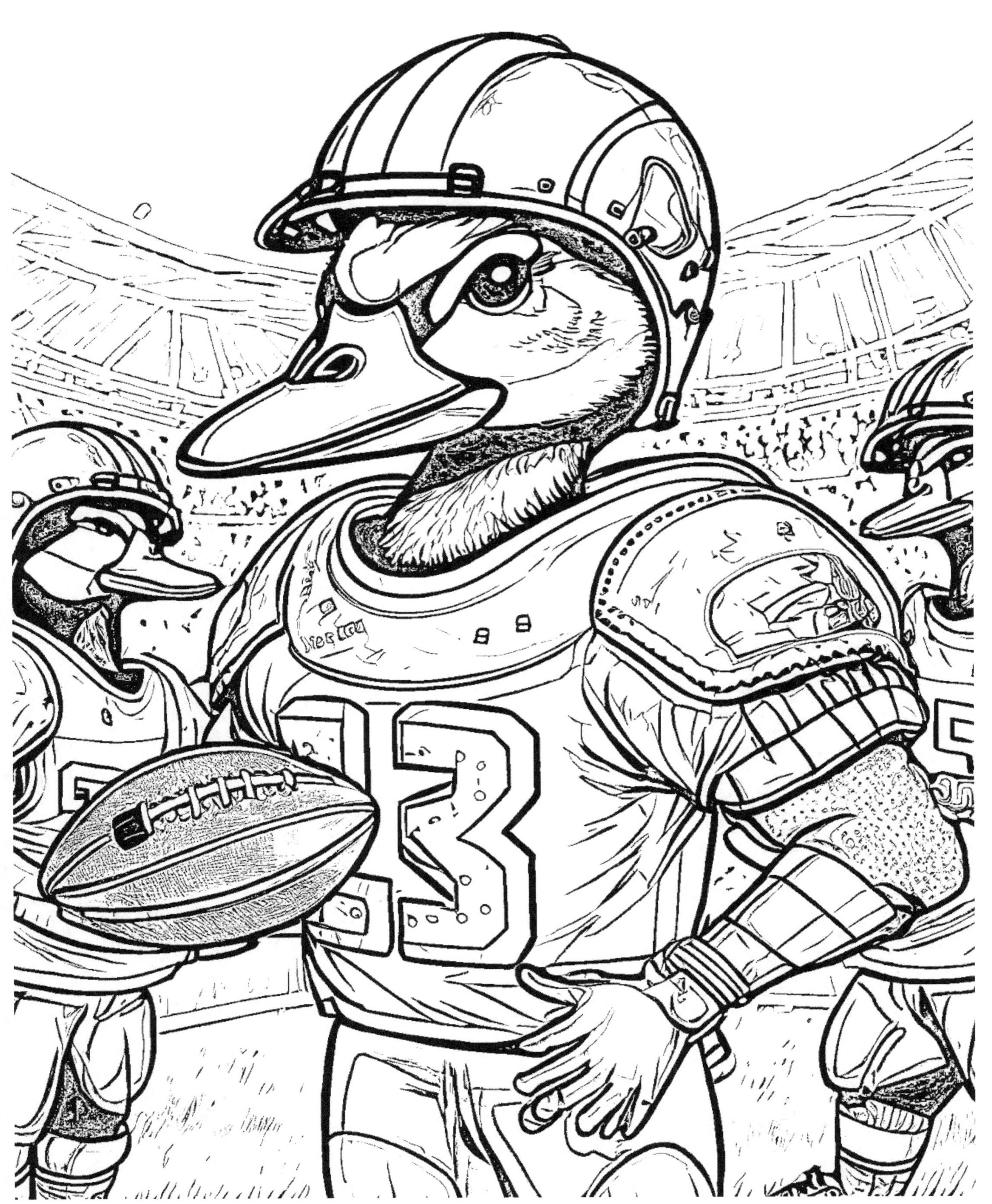

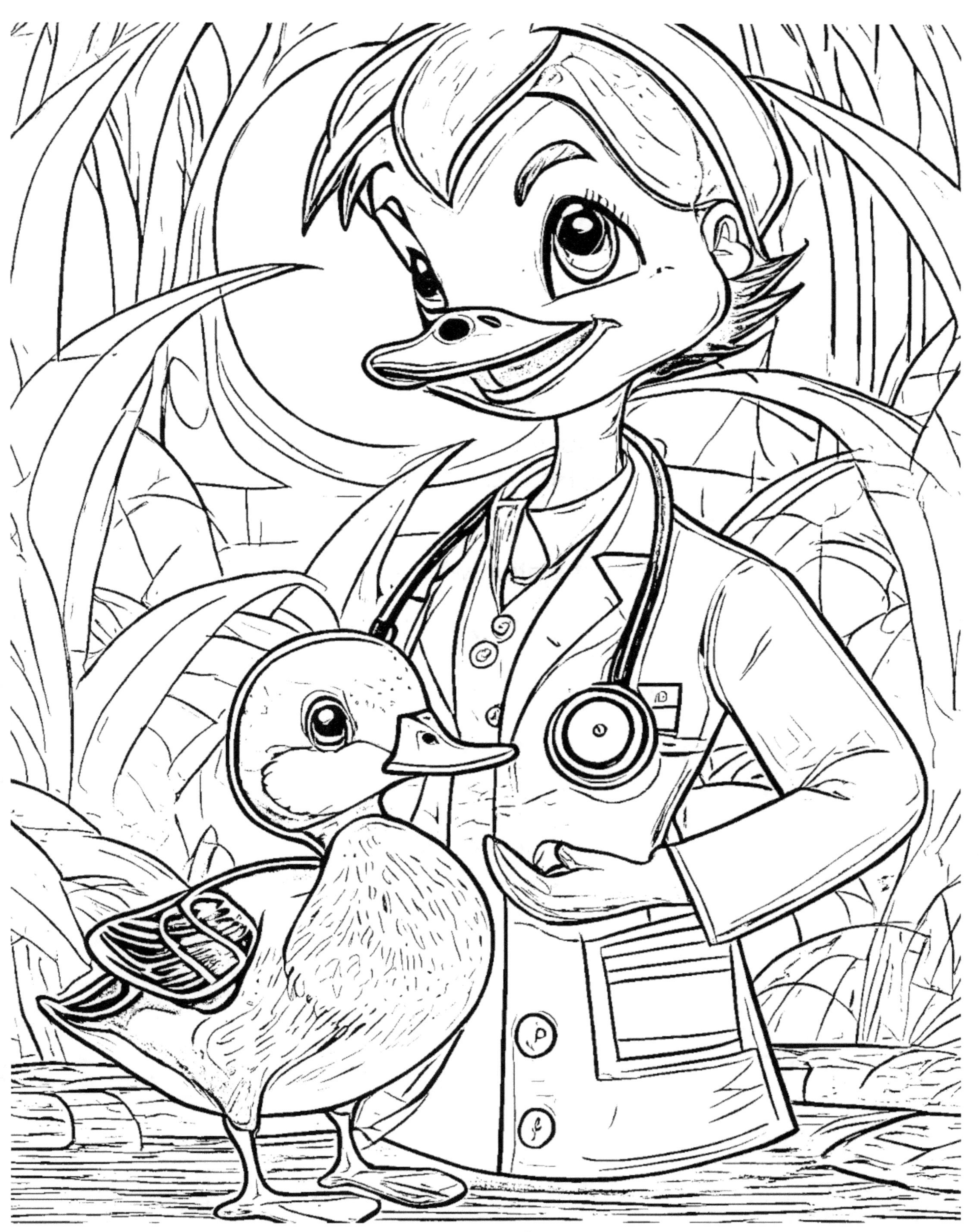

Written and Illustrated by Brandon Bishop
& Ronald Kotynski

In association with ASY TV

WATCH ASY TV AT ASYTV.COM

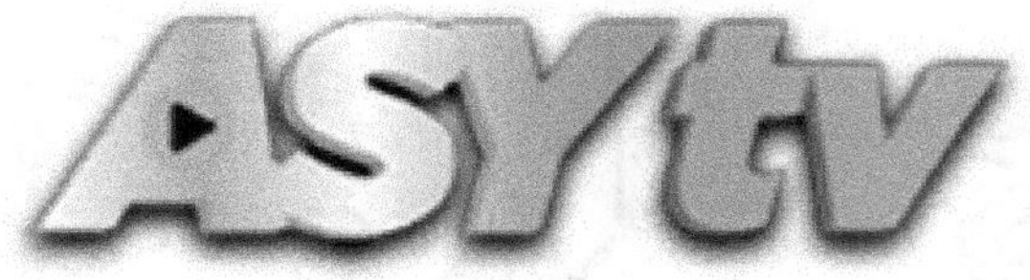

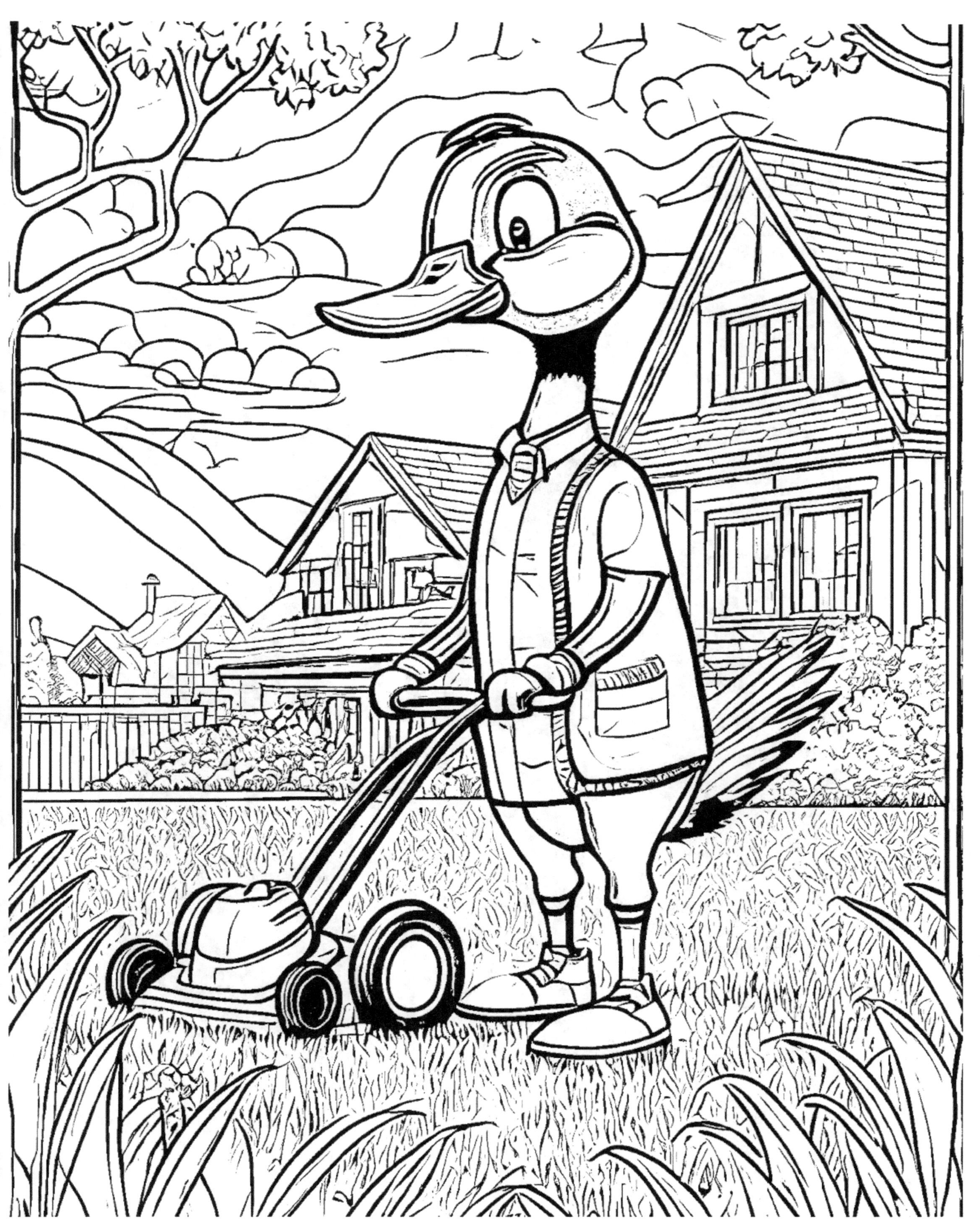

Also available:

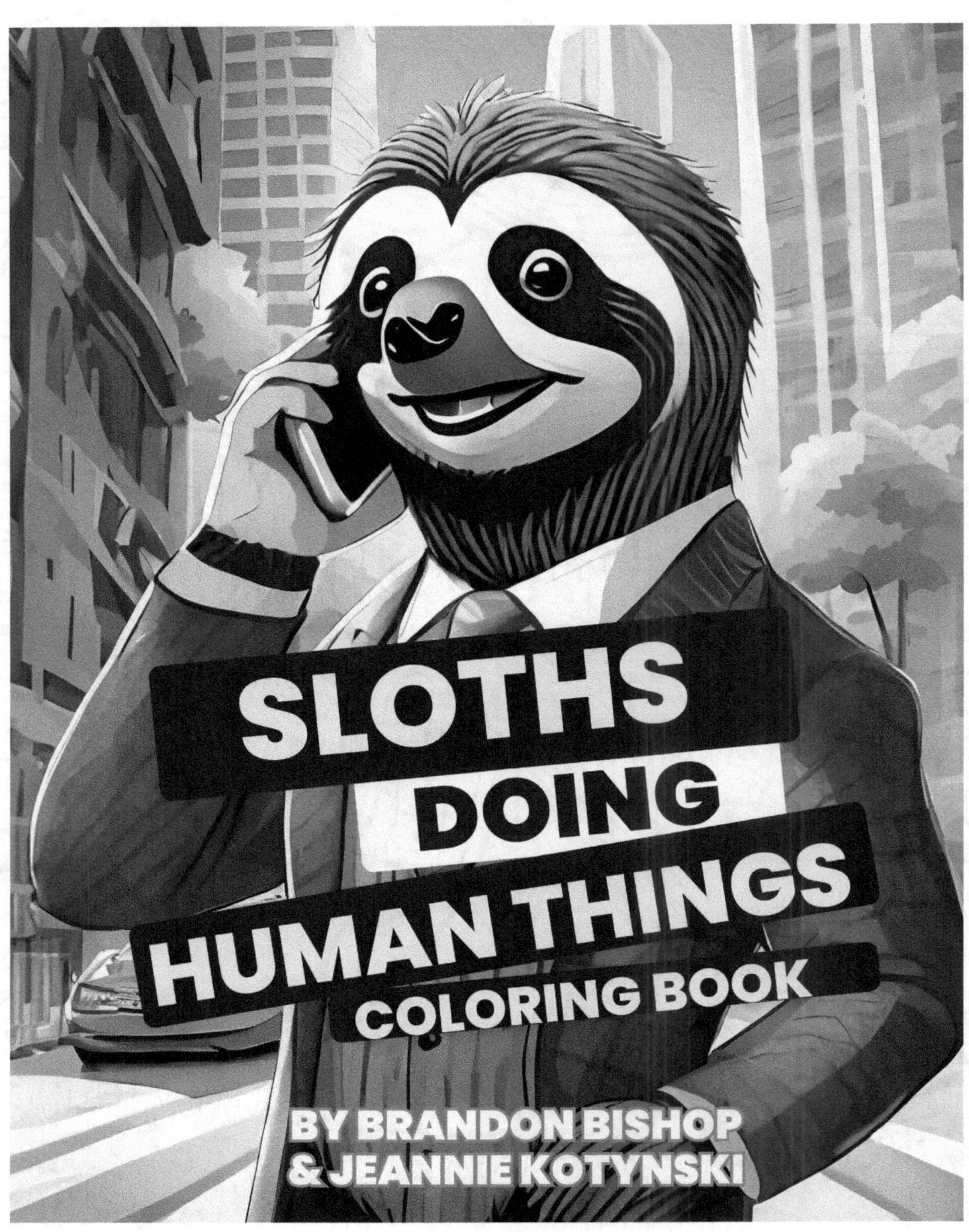